HAWAI'I'S FLOWER LEIS

An Identification Guide to over 50 of Hawai'i's Favorite Leis

LAURIE SHIMIZU IDE

Second Printing, August 2010

Design by Sistenda Yim

ISBN-10: 1-56647-530-9
ISBN-13: 978-1-56647-530-3

Mutual Publishing, LLC
1215 Center Street, Suite 210
Honolulu, Hawai'i 96816
Ph: (808) 732-1709
Fax: (808) 734-4094
e-mail: info@mutualpublishing.com
www.mutualpublishing.com

Printed in Korea

MAHALO ME KE ALOHA PUMEHANA

—Thank You with Warmest Love and Affection—

Toshi & Ethel Shimizu
Elaine Mezurashi
Barney Bareng
Clara Tamura
Yukio & Audrey Toguchi
Vernon Abe
Paradise Florist
Flo's Min Florist
Mylene's Floral Wholesale
Sets Kataoka
Floy Kaku
Jean Ishimoto
Michele Nagafuchi
Heidi Leianuenue Bornhorst
Jan McEwen
Art Buckman
Bernie & Cristy Cagauan
The Staff at Photo Trends – Pearlridge
Howard Hamada

Most of all, my sincere thank you to my
husband, Karl, and daughter, Karley,
who have to deal with
everything flowers,
flowers,
flowers,
every day.

TABLE OF CONTENTS

AUTHOR'S PREFACE

There are many ways to string a lei.
No one way is the "correct" way.
Each individual must discover what
feels and looks best.

The quantities of blossoms listed may
vary depending on the size of the
blossoms.

The lei life is based on the
average life of the flower when
stored properly.

Because of the "one-day wearing" lei life…

A LEI IS TO BE WORN,

ADORED BY EYES,

AND CHERISHED IN HEARTS.

The Hawaiian flower lei, known worldwide, is by far the most beautiful token of our "aloha spirit" in the Islands. Aloha means love, hello, goodbye, friendship and affection—all of the reasons to give a lei. A lei is usually presented with a kiss, which represents love, a wish of luck, admiration for loved ones, warmth and friendship. This custom is now universally known as the "Hawaiian lei custom."

Back in the Boat Days of the late 1800s and early 1900s, visitors arriving or leaving on steamboats each received a lei as a gift of aloha. It is said that departing visitors would throw their leis into the sea as the ships passed Diamond Head in hopes of the lei floating back to Hawai'i's beaches. This would signify that he or she would return to the Islands someday. Today, the giving of a lei to someone who is arriving or departing the Islands continues, but the lei is often kept for its beauty, fragrance and special memories.

In old Hawai'i, the lei was created as a symbol to honor the gods, loved ones and oneself. Leis were made with flowers, leaves, seeds, nuts, shells, bone, wood and even human hair. They were made for the head *(lei po'o)*, the neck *(lei 'ā'ī)*, or the wrist and ankles *(kūpe'e)*.

Today, the most common length is a 40-inch lei made for the neck *(lei 'a'i)*. Leis are given for birthdays, anniversaries, weddings, graduations, lū'au, funerals, Mother's Day, Father's Day, Secretary's Day, Easter, Valentine's Day, to visitors arriving and leaving the Islands, to teachers, newscasters, coaches, anyone celebrating a special occasion, and also to oneself on "Aloha Fridays." A lei may also be worn for no special occasion, simply to feel and express our magical "aloha spirit."

Over the years, new materials and techniques have been introduced into this ancient art form, creating unlimited lei designs. A flower lei may be combined with nuts, seeds, shells, beads, ribbons, and currency. Specialty leis are also made with candy, cookies, golf balls, fabric, ribbon and anything else imaginable.

This book is intended to be a visual guide of the floral leis you see and receive in Hawai'i. I hope it helps you identify those special leis given to you, and that you keep the warm memories of receiving them.

A Symbolic Lei For Every Island

NI'IHAU
"The Kapu Isle"

Pūpū Shells
Momi: *Euplica varians* • Laiki: *Mitrella margarita*
Kahelelani: *Leptothyra verruca*

KAUAʻI
"The Garden Isle"

Mokihana:
Pelea anisata

O'AHU
"The Gathering Place"

'Ilima:
Sida fallax

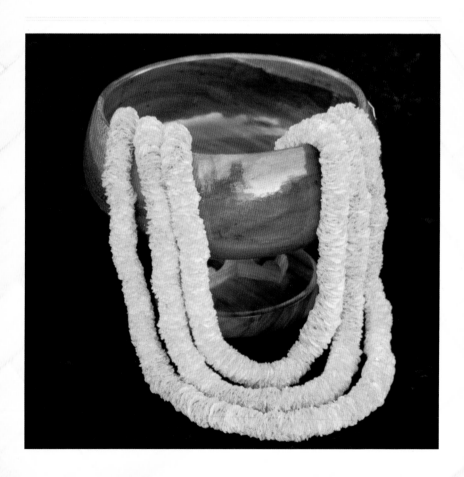

MOLOKAʻI
"The Friendly Isle"

Kukui or Candlenut:
Aleurites moluccana

LĀNAʻI
"The Secluded Isle"

Kaunaʻoa Kahakai or Hawaiian Dodder:
Cuscota sandwichiana

MAUI
"The Magic Isle"

Lokelani:
Rosa chinensis

KAHOʻOLAWE
"The Barren Isle"

Hinahina Kū Kahakai:
Heliotropium anomalum var. argenteum

HAWAI'I
"The Orchid Isle" or "The Big Isle"

'Ōhi'a Lehua:
Metrosideros collina subsp. *polymorphia*

Lei-Making Needles

A modern addition to the art of lei making, metal needles have greatly expanded what types of leis may be made. The ancient Hawaiians did not have metals, thus no needles.

A long, stainless steel needle (often made in Hawai'i) can be found at a florist or craft center.

This special needle is sharpened to a point at one end, while the other end is bent to a flat "eye" to hook on the thread. After threading, this "eye" must be flat so that blossoms can slide over it smoothly, preventing breakage.

The needles used in lei making vary in length and thickness. They range from 3″ to 14″ in length, and are available in thin, medium and thick grades.

The most common stainless steel needle used for stringing a lei is the 12″ long, medium-grade needle.

Six Lei-Making Methods

1. Kui—stringing

a. Kui pololei—
straight, single pattern

b. Kui poepoe—
circular, double pattern

c. Kui lau—
back-and-forth pattern

2. Hili or **hilo**—
braiding, weaving
pattern

3. Wili—twining, twisting pattern

4. Humuhumu papa or
humupapa —sewing
with a needle and thread

5. Haku—setting or
mounting against a
background material

**6. Kīpuʻu, hīpuʻu,
nīpuʻu**—tying together,
knotted pattern

ʻĀkulikuli

Translation: Succulent • Common Name: Ice Plant or Noon Flower • Scientific Name: *Lampranthus glomeratus* (shining flower with a rounded cluster shape) • Family Name: Carpetweed (Aizoaceae)

Description: A ground cover succulent with blossoms ranging from white, to pink, red, yellow, and orange; spiky blossoms about 1″ long and 2″ wide, with numerous fine petals and stamens; no fragrance.

Characteristics: Flowers open at around noon in sunshine and close in the evening. One to four days lei life.

Climate/Location: Tropical climate, near salt marshes or brackish water, usually in low-lying areas near the shore; direct sunlight. Abundant in Waimea on the Big Island of Hawaiʻi, and in Hoʻolehua, Maui.

Season/Harvest Period: Year-round, abundant from April to October. Pick buds early in the morning. Keep out of water to preserve soft, pliable stems. String blossoms in the bud stage. To blossom, leave lei out of the refrigerator for about two hours. The blossoms will open and interlace, creating a full lei.

Quantity: About 550 blossoms for a 40″, strung by fours, half-circular, double lei.

Storage: Keep dry and airtight. Wrap in dry tissue or paper towel. Place in plastic bag or container. Refrigerate.

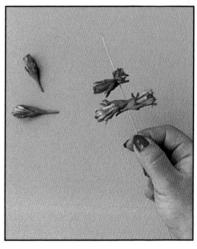

Alahe'e Haole
or
Walahe'e Haole

Translation: Mock Orange • Common Name: Mock Orange or Orange Jasmine • Scientific Name: *Murraya paniculata* (orange jessamine, having flowers arranged in panicles) Synonym: *Murraya exotica* • Family Name: Rue (Rutaceae)

Description: An ornamental hedge plant with shiny, dark-green leaves and small white flowers. Strong fragrance.

Characteristics: The leaves are what is used for lei making. One to seven days lei life. The flowers are fragile.

Climate/Location: Warm climate; backyard cultivation and hedges around parks and playgrounds; direct sunlight.

Season/Harvest Period: Year-round for its leaves. Blossoms June through December. Pick leaves when they are a dark green.

Quantity: About 1,200 leaves for a 40″ double lei, *kui poepoe,* circular pattern.

Storage: Keep dry and airtight. Place in a plastic bag. Refrigerate.

Aloalo Pahūpahū

Translation: Firecracker Hibiscus • Common Name: Firecracker Hibiscus, Turk's Cap, Lei Hibiscus or Hanging Hibiscus • Scientific Name: *Malvaviscus penduliflorus* (mallow-glue, hanging flowers) Synonym. *Malvaviscus arobreus var. penduliflorus* • Family Name: Hibiscus (Malvaceae)

Description: A shrub with firecracker red, 2″ to 2-1/2″ long, pendant blossoms which do not open; protruding stamens; no fragrance.

Characteristics: Bright red, eye-catching color. One day lei life.

Climate/Location: Warm climate; tropical region; backyard cultivation; direct sunlight.

Season/Harvest Period: Year-round, low during December through February. Pick when mature in size, before blossoms "loosen" open.

Quantity: About 90 blossoms for a 40″ Micronesian-style lei, flat, weaving pattern. (A lei style originating from Micronesia).

Storage: Keep dry and airtight. Roll or fold into a ball. Wrap in wax paper. Refrigerate.

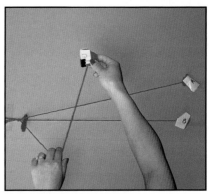

'Awapuhi Ke'oke'o

Translation: White Ginger • Common Name: White Ginger • Scientific Name: *Hedychium coronarium* (ginger-lily for garlands) • Family Name: Ginger (Zingiberaceae)

Description: A leaf stalk bearing white blossoms; 3″ diameter; shaped like a moth; 1-1/2″ long with a broad lip at the top and a pair of side petals. Strong fragrance.

Characteristics: The fragrance lasts for two days. One day lei life.

Climate/Location: Warm to cool climate; grows wild along streams and damp, cool roadsides and forests; backyard cultivation; direct sunlight.

Season/Harvest Period: Year-round, peaking late spring to late fall. Micronesian (braiding or weaving pattern)—pick blossoms as buds. Rinse off any insect pests. Gently shake off excess water. Do not place in water; keep in bud form. Wrap in ti leaf. Place in cellophane wrap; keep airtight. Refrigerate. Buds may be stored several days until enough buds are gathered.

Quantity: About 120 buds for a 40″ Micronesian lei, flat, braiding and weaving pattern (a lei style originating from Micronesia).

Storage: The Micronesian-style lei may be rolled into a ball. Keep dry and airtight in plastic wrap. Refrigerate.

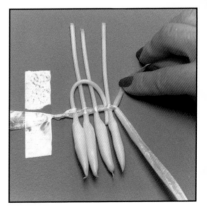

Hala

Translation: To pass, a new beginning or fault • Common Name: Screw Pine, Walking Tree, or Pineapple Tree • Scientific Name: *Pandanus tectorius* (screw-pine, derived from tectorum—of the roofs of houses) Synonym. *Pandanus odoratissimus* • Family Name: Screw Pine (Pandanaceae)

Description: A tree bearing pineapple like fragrant fruits, 8″ to 10″ in diameter, turning green to yellow, and then orange when ripe.

Characteristics: The fruit may carry insect pests. The Federal Department of Agriculture prohibits taking this fruit to the Mainland. The fruits are found only on female trees; male trees produce blossoms called "hinano" that were used as an aphrodisiac by ancient Hawaiians. One to five days lei life.

Climate/Location: Warm climate; low elevation; moist coastal areas; direct sunlight.

Season/Harvest Period: Year-round. Pick fruit when it is light green to light yellow. Cut when the center turns bright yellow or orange in color.

Quantity: About 55 keys for a 40″ single lei, *kui pololei,* straight pattern. Lauaʻe leaves *(Microsorium scolopendria)* may be added between each key.

Storage: Keep dry. Place in plastic bag or container. Refrigerate.

He'e

Translation: Octopus • Common Name: Octopus Tree, Umbrella Tree • Scientific Name: *Schefflera actinophylla* (named for botanist J.C. Scheffler, flannel flower at the edge of leaf branches) Synonym. *Brassaia actinophylla* • Family Name: Panax (Araliaceae)

Description: A tree with round clusters of flower buds, turning pink to red to brown; located on spikes, like the arms of an octopus. No fragrance.

Characteristics: Durable. Up to ten days lei life.

Climate/Location: Tropical climate; backyard cultivation; along roadsides; in wet forests; direct sunlight.

Season/Harvest Period: Year-round, peaking April through October. Pick bud cluster before they blossom; pink and red buds are favorable.

Quantity: About 85 clusters for a 40″ single lei, *kui pololei,* straight pattern.

Storage: Keep dry. Wrap in newspaper. Refrigerate.

Hinahina or 'Umi 'Umi O Dole

Translation: Grayish beard or whiskers of Mr. Dole • Common Name: Spanish Moss, Dole's Beard or Whiskers, Florida Moss, Pele's Hair • Scientific Name: *Tillandsia usneoides* (Spanish moss, resembling usnes, a lichen that looks like Spanish moss) • Family Name: Pineapple (Bromeliaceae)

Description: Slender, grayish, thread-like moss that grows on tree branches. No fragrance.

Characteristics: Represented as a substitute for the true Hinahina of Kaho'olawe, Hinahina Kū Kahakai *(Heliotropium anomalum var. argenteum).* Up to 14 days lei life.

Climate/Location: Warm climate; backyard cultivation; direct or indirect sunlight.

Season/Harvest Period: Year-round. Harvest any time.

Quantity: At one's discretion.

Storage: Store at room temperature or refrigerate.

Hōkū Hihi

Translation: Star-shaped, vine • Common Name: Hoya, Star Flower, Wax Flower or Wax Plant • Scientific Name: *Hoya carnosa* (climbing flowering evergreen plants named for Thomas Hoy, fleshy) • Family Name: Milkweed (Asclepiadaceae)

Description: A vine climbing by its roots with white, waxy, 1/2″ diameter blossoms with a pink center. The fragrant flowers are star-shaped in clusters.

Characteristics: Fairly long-lasting. One to five days lei life.

Climate/Location: Warm climate; backyard cultivation on fences; direct sunlight.

Season/Harvest Period: Blossoms during the winter through summer. Pick blossoms when they are fully opened.

Quantity: About 200 blossoms for a 40″ single lei, *kui pololei,* straight pattern.

Storage: Place in a plastic bag or container. Refrigerate.

'Ilima Aloalo Pele

Translation: Bell Hibiscus • Common Name: Lantern Ilima, Bell Ilima or Abutilon • Scientific Name: *Abutilon pictum* (flowering maple, brightly painted) • Family Name: Hibiscus (Malvaceae)

Description: A shrub with bell-shaped, yellow-orange with red veins; 1″ long blossoms with a bright red center; no fragrance.

Characteristics: Fairly long-lasting. One to three days lei life.

Climate/Location: Warm climate; backyard cultivation; direct sunlight.

Season/Harvest Period: Year-round, peaks in the summer. Pick when blossoms are half opened to fully opened. Blossoms will open as you string them.

Quantity: About 75 blossoms for a single lei, *kui pololei,* straight pattern.

Storage: Keep dry. Place in plastic bag or container. Refrigerate.

'Ilima Aloalo Papa

Translation: Forbidden Hibiscus • Common Name: 'Ilima or Royal 'Ilima • Scientific Name: *Sida fallax* (water plant, deceptive) • Family Name: Hibiscus (Malvaceae)

Description: A shrub with delicate, tissue paper-like flowers, light to deep yellow in color; 1" in diameter with five petals; no fragrance.

Characteristics: Flower of O'ahu; lei of royalty; fragile. One day lei life.

Climate/Location: Warm climate; backyard cultivation; low elevation; direct sunlight.

Season/Harvest Period: Year-round, peaking in the summer. To prevent bruising, pick in bud form before sunrise, no later than early mid-morning. Flowers open to full bloom by noon.

Quantity: About 700 blossoms for a single lei, *kui pololei,* straight pattern.

Storage: Keep dry and airtight. Wrap in dry tissue paper or paper towel. Place in a plastic container or bag. Refrigerate.

'Ilima Aloalo Ma'o

Translation: Green Hibiscus • Common Name: Royal 'Ilima or Hairy Abutilon • Scientific Name: *Abutilon grandifolium* (flowering maple, sweet and big) • Family Name: Hibiscus (Malvaceae)

Discription: A shrub with light orange, 1″ in diameter, delicate, paper-like double-petalled blossom with a large green calyx; no fragrance.

Charactieristic: Fragile. One day lei life.

Climate/Location: Warm climate; backyard cultivation; low elevation; direct sunlight.

Season/Harvest Period: Year-round, peaking in the summer. Pick when fully blossomed in the mid-morning through early afternoon. Flowers are best when picked fully opened.

Quantity: About 130 blossoms for a 40″ single lei, *kui pololei,* straight pattern.

Storage: Keep dry and airtight. Wrap in dry tissue or paper towel. Place in a plastic bag or container. Refrigerate.

Kākia

Translation: Cassia • Common Name: Candle Bush or Akapulko • Scientific Name: *Senna alata* (cassia, winged) Synonym. *Cassia alata* • Family Name: Bean (Fabaceae)

Description: A shrub with yellow, 1″ flowers; 5 petals closely packed on a spike. No fragrance.

Characteristics: Blossoms may carry microscopic insect pests. The Federal Department of Agriculture prohibits taking this flower to the Mainland. Fragile. One day lei life.

Climate/Location: Tropical climate; wet lowlands; backyard cultivation; direct sunlight.

Season/Harvest Period: Late winter through early summer. Pick blossoms in the morning before they blossom.

Quanity: About 450 blossoms for a 40″ double lei, *kui poepoe,* circular pattern.

Storage: Keep dry. Refrigerate.

Kalaunu

Translation: Crown • Common Name: Crown Flower • Scientific Name: *Calotropis gigantea* (beautiful ship, unusually tall or large) • Family Name: Milkweed (Asciepiadaceae)

Description: A shrub with pale lavender or white blossoms, 1-1/2″ in diameter, with 5 curled-back petals around a waxy crown; light fragrance.

Characteristics: Milk sap, in large doses, is extremely toxic; remove sap from skin, preventing irritation. Versatile lei styles; one to three days lei life. (Use hand lotion before picking and stringing to prevent sap from sticking.)

Climate/Location: Warm climate; backyard cultivation; direct sunlight.

Season/Harvest Period: Year-round, peaking in the summer. Pick the blossoms in the early or mid-morning when cool.

Quantity: About 65 blossoms for a 40″ single lei, *kui pololei,* straight pattern.

Storage: Keep dry and airtight. Place in a plastic bag or container. Refrigerate.

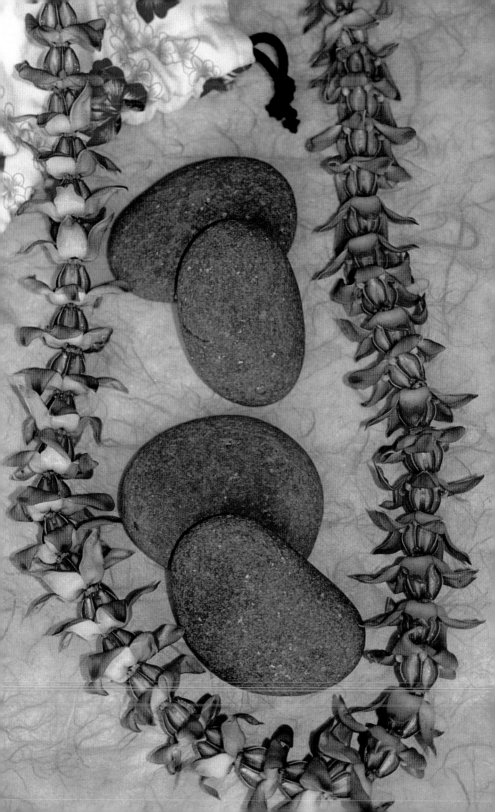

Kalaunu (Iki)

Translation: Small Crown • Common Name: Small Crown, Dwarf Crown or Giant Milkweed • Scientific Name: *Calotropis procera* (beautiful ship, tall) • Family Name: Milkweed (Asclepiadaceae)

Description: A shrub with pale lavender blossoms about 1″ in diameter, with 5 petals around, a waxy, short crown; light fragrance.

Characteristics: Milk sap, in large doses, is extremely toxic; remove sap from skin, preventing iritation. One to three days lei life.

Climate/Location: Warm climate; backyard cultivation; direct sunlight.

Season/Harvest Period: Year-round, peaking in the summer. Pick the blossoms in the early or mid-morning when cool.

Quantity: About 120 crowns for a 40″ single lei, *kui pololei,* straight pattern.

Storage: Keep dry and airtight. Place in a plastic bag or container. Refrigerate.

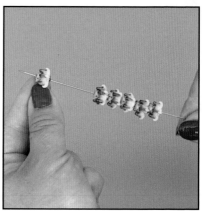

Kamaloli

Translation: Snail • Common Name: Snail Vine, Snail Bean or Corkscrew Flower • Scientific Name: *Vigna caracalla* (twining herb, named after a Roman Emperor) Synonym: *Phaseolus caracalla* or *Phaseolus gigantea* • Family Name: Bean (Fabaceae)

Description: A fast-growing, perennial vine up to 20' long. Flowers are light lavender, about 2″ in diameter with a twisted, disfigured shape. Mild fragrance.

Characteristics: Fragile. One day lei life.

Climate/Location: Warm climate; backyard cultivation; direct sunlight.

Season/Harvest Period: Year-round; low during winter. Pick blossoms in the early morning when cool.

Quantity: About 80 blossoms for a 40″ double lei, *kui poepoe,* circular pattern.

Storage: Keep dry and airtight. Place in a plastic bag or container. Refrigerate.

Kauhi or ʻĀwikiwiki or Maunaloa

Translation: ʻĀwikiwiki – swift; Maunaloa – sea bean • Common Name: True Maunaloa • Scientific Name: *Canavalia cathartica* (jack-bean, purgative) Synonym. *Canavalia microcarpa* • Family Name: Bean (Fabaceae)

Description: A vine with pink or lavender, 1″ to 1-1/2″ long, pea-like blossoms; mild fragrance.

Characteristics: Seed attached to the blossoms may carry microscopic insect pests. The Federal Department of Agriculture prohibits this flower from entering the Mainland. One to three days lei life.

Climate/Location: Warm lowlands; backyard cultivation; direct sunlight.

Season/Harvest Period: Year-round, peaking in May through October. Pick blossoms when fully opened.

Quantity: About 165 blossoms for a double lei, *kui poepoe,* circular pattern.

Storage: Keep dry and airtight. Place in a plastic bag or plastic container. Refrigerate.

Kauna'oa Kahakai

Translation: Beach Orphan Vine • Common Name: Dodder • Scientific Name: *Cuscuta sandwichiana* (dodder, tangled twist of hair, from the Sandwich Islands) • Family Name: Morning Glory (Convolvulaceae)

Description: A yellow-orange parasitic vine, leafless, entwining, with tiny white blossoms; no fragrance.

Characteristics: The Kauna'oa lei represents the island of Lāna'i. One to five days lei life.

Climate/Location: Warm climate; along roadsides, beaches, and uncultivated fields, growing and twining over plants and even up trees; direct sunlight.

Season/Harvest Period: Year-round. Pick any time.

Quantity: At one's discretion.

Storage: Do not sprinkle. Refrigerate.

Kenikeni

Translation: Ten-Cent or Dime • Common Name: Pua Kenikeni, Ten-Cent Flower • Scientific Name: *Fagraea berterana* (named after J. Th. Fagracus; named after Botanist C.G.L. Bertero) • Family Name: Logania (Loganiaceae)

Description: A tree producing 2″ long, 5-petalled, white, tubular blossoms; changes to yellow, then orange; strong perfume fragrance.

Characteristics: The flower has been called the "ten-cent flower" since the "Steamer Days" of the late 1800s and early 1900s. It is rumored that the blossoms were so prized, a Pua Kenikeni lei sold for ten cents. One to three days lei life.

Climate/Location: Warm climate; backyard cultivation; direct sunlight.

Season/Harvest Period: Seasonal from April through November. Pick the blossoms in the early morning or evening when cool.

Quantity: About 45 blossoms for a 40″ single lei, *kui pololei,* straight pattern.

Storage: Keep dry and cool. Place the lei in an air-filled plastic bag; float the bag in a container of water; keep at room temperature; do not refrigerate.

Kepalo or Pukanawila

Translation: Devil or Bougainvillea • Common Name: Bougainvillea • Scientific Name: *Bougainvillea* spp. (named in honor of Louis Antoine de Bougainville) • Family Name: Four O'Clock (Nyctagineceae)

Description: A shrub with paper-like blossoms, 1″ to 2″ in length, made up of three colorful modified leaves called bracts in a triangular cup form, holding three small, whitish-yellow tubular flowers; no fragrance.

Characteristics: Available in various colors. One to three days lei life.

Climate/Location: Tropical, warm climate; backyard cultivation; along roadsides; direct sunlight.

Season/Harvest Period: Year-round, peaking in the summer. Pick the blossoms in the morning or evening when cool.

Quantity: About 75 blossoms for a 40″ double lei, *kui poepoe,* circular pattern.

Storage: Sprinkle lightly; gently shake off excess water. Place in a plastic bag or container. Refrigerate.

Kiele

Translation: Gardenia • Common Name: Gardenia or Cape Jasmine • Scientific Name: *Gardenia jasminoides* or *Gardenia augusta* (named after Alexander Garden, resembling jasmine) • Family Name: Coffee (Rubiaceae)

Description: A shrub with white, 3-4″ diameter blossoms with a long, tubular corolla, 5-point long winged calyx; strong fragrance.

Characteristics: The blossom attracts insect pests. The Federal Department of Agriculture pro-hibits transporting this flower or its foliage to the Mainland. One day lei life.

Climate/Location: Warm climate; backyard cultivation; direct sun-light.

Season/Harvest Period: March through June; occasionally pro-ducing a few blossoms in the fall. Pick the blossoms in the morning in the bud stage to reduce bruis-ing. Place buds in water to open.

Quantity: About 40 blossoms for a 40″ single lei, *kui pololei,* straight pattern.

Storage: Sprinkle lightly. Store on wet paper in a bowl, un-wrapped. Refrigerate.

Kiele (Peke)

Translation: Dwarf Gardenia • Common Name: Dwarf Gardenia or Cape Jasmine • Scientific Name: *Gardenia augusta 'Radicans'* (named after Alexander Garden, resembling jasmine, having rooting stems) • Family Name: Coffee (Rubiaceae)

Description: A shrub with white, 2″ diameter blossoms with a long, tubular corolla; mild fragrance.

Characteristics: The blossom attracts insect pests. The Federal Department of Agriculture prohibits transporting this flower or its foliage to the Mainland. One day lei life.

Climate/Location: Warm climate; backyard cultivation; direct sunlight.

Season/Harvest Period: May through July; occasionally producing a few blossoms in the fall. Pick the blossoms fully opened in the morning when it is cool.

Quantity: About 100 blossoms for a 40″ single lei, *kui pololei,* straight pattern.

Storage: Sprinkle lightly. Store on paper towel in a bowl, unwrapped. Refrigerate.

Kīkā

Translation: Cigar • Common Name: Cigar • Scientific Name: *Cuphea ignea* (curved, fiery red) • Family Name: Crape Myrtle (Lythraceae)

Description: A shrub with 3/4" long, tubular, slender orange-red blossoms with black 6-tipped teeth, white-speck mouth; resembles a miniature lit cigar tipped with white ash; no fragrance.

Characteristics: Very long-lasting; popular to ship to the Mainland. Up to 14 days lei life.

Climate/Location: Tropical, warm climate; backyard cultivation; direct sunlight.

Season/Harvest Period: Year-round; blooms in intervals throughout the year; less in the hot summer months, July through August. Pick blossoms in the early morning or evening when cool. The flowers are soft during the mid-day.

Quantity: About 1,800 blossoms for a 40" double lei, *kui poepoe*, circular pattern.

Storage: Sprinkle lightly. Place in plastic bag or container. Refrigerate. May be revived by soaking in cold water in the refrigerator for four hours. Shake off excess water. Place in a plastic bag. Refrigerate.

Kīkānia

Translation: Noxious Weed • Common Name: Solanum or Nightshade • Scientific name: *Solanum aculeatissimum* (varied genus for the potato, Jerusalem cherry and woody nightshade, very pricky) Synonym. *Solanum capsicoides* • Family Name: Nightshade (Solanaceae)

Description: A shrub with round, reddish-orange fruits, approximately 1″ in diameter; dry; containing winged seeds. No fragrance.

Characteristics: The fruit is poisonous if eaten. The Federal Department of Agriculture prohibits transporting this fruit to the Mainland. One to seven days lei life.

Climate/Location: Warm climate; backyard cultivation; direct sunlight.

Season/Harvest Period: Year-round. Harvest when fruit is bright orange.

Quantity: About 45 fruits for a 40″ single lei, *kui pololei,* straight pattern.

Storage: Keep dry. Place in plastic bag or container. Refrigerate.

Kukui

Translation: Lamp, light, or torch • Common Name: Kukui or Candlenut •
Scientific Name: *Aleurites moluccana* (floury, dusted with flour, from Moluccas
or Spice Islands of Indonesia) • Family Name: Spurge (Euphorbiaceae)

Description: A tree with angular-pointed, silvery, pale-green leaves with whitish down covering; small, white blossoms arranged in clusters; mild fragrance. The fruit contains a white nut when immature, black when ripe.

Characteristics: The Kukui tree is named the official tree emblem for the State of Hawai‘i because of the multiplicity of its uses by the ancient Hawaiians, i.e., light, fuel, medicine, and dye. The leaf lei has a one to four days lei life. The nut lei (not shown) has an everlasting lei life. The kukui lei represent the island of Moloka‘i.

Climate/Location: Tropical; warm climate; low mountain elevation; direct sunlight.

Season/Harvest Period: Year-round. Pick the leaves and blossoms during cool morning or evening hours.

Quantity: About 150 small to medium size leaves for a 60″ open-ended, horseshoe lei, *haku,* setting and mounting pattern. Flowers and nuts can be used at one's discretion.

Storage: Sprinkle lightly. Place in plastic bag or container. Refrigerate.

Kukuna-O-Ka-Lā

Translation: Rays of the Sun • Common Name: Oriental Mangrove • Scientific Name: *Bruguiera gymnorhiza* (named in honor of G. Bruguiere, naked root) Syn. *Bruguiera conjugata* • Family Name: Mangrove (Rhizophoraceae)

Description: A tree with pink, yellow, or red blossoms; calyx has about 10 erect bristle lobes, longer than the petals, about 20 stamens; no fragrance.

Characteristics: The lei is made with the strong calyx of the blossoms. Up to ten days lei life.

Climate/Location: Warm climate; found in tropical and subtropical seacoasts and marshes, in the mouths of streams; direct sunlight.

Season/Harvest Period: Year-round. Harvest any time. Only the calyx is used for the lei.

Quantity: About 85 calyces for a 40″ single lei, *kui pololei,* straight pattern.

Storage: Submerge in cold water; gently shake off excess water. Place in a plastic bag or container. Refrigerate.

Kupaloke or Kupalo

Translation: Tuberose • Common Name: Tuberose • Scientific Name: *Polianthes tuberosa* (grey, whitish flower, tuberous) • Family Name: Amaryllis (Amaryllidaceae)

Description: A plant with grass-like leaves, with 2″ elongated white blossoms with spreading, oblong petals; strong fragrance.

Characteristics: Popular among visitors for its fragrance. One to two days lei life.

Climate/Location: Warm climate; backyard cultivation; direct sunlight.

Season/Harvest Period: Year-round, peaking February through October. Pick the fully-opened blossoms in the morning or evening when it is cool.

Quantity: About 45 blossoms for a 40″ single lei, *kui pololei,* straight pattern.

Storage: Keep dry. Place in paper or plastic bag. Refrigerate.

Lā'ī or Ki

Translation: Peaceful • Common Name: Ti Leaf or Ki Leaf • Scientific Name: *Cordyline fruticosa* (a club, dwarf and shrubby) Syn. *Cordyline terminalis* • Family Name: Agave (Agavaceae)

Description: A plant with narrow, oblong, smooth, shiny, flexible leaves; 1 to 2 feet long; approximately 4″ wide, growing in a spiral cluster.

Characteristics: Plants and leaves are believed to ward off evil spirits and bring good luck. The leaves are used for leis. Up to seven days lei life. Also used as a dried lei. The flowers are fragile.

Climate/Location: Warm climate; backyard cultivation; direct or indirect sunlight.

Season/Harvest Period: Year-round; pick the mature leaves; harvest any time.

Quantity: About 13 large leaves for a 60″ open-ended, horseshoe lei, *wili*, twining, twisting pattern.

Storage: Keep dry. Wrap in newspaper. Refrigerate.

Lehua Pepa
or
Lei-Hua Mau Loa

Translation: Paper Lehua, Everlasting Lehua • Common Name: Bozu, Globe Amaranth, or Paper Ball • Scientific Name: *Gomphrena globosa* (globe amaranth) • Family Name: Amaranth (Amaranthaceae)

Description: A shrub with 3/4″ diameter, ball-shaped, paper-like blossoms in white, violet, pink, or purple. Each blossom has 2 leafy bracts; no fragrance.

Characteristics: Long-lasting lei. Up to seven days lei life; also can be used as a dried lei.

Climate/Location: Warm climate; backyard cultivation; direct sunlight.

Season/Harvest Period: Year-round. Pick blossoms in the early morning or evening when cool.

Quantity: About 280 blossoms for a double lei, *kui poepoe,* circular pattern.

Storage: Keep dry. Wrap in a paper towel or newspaper. Refrigerate to keep fresh. To dry, do not refrigerate.

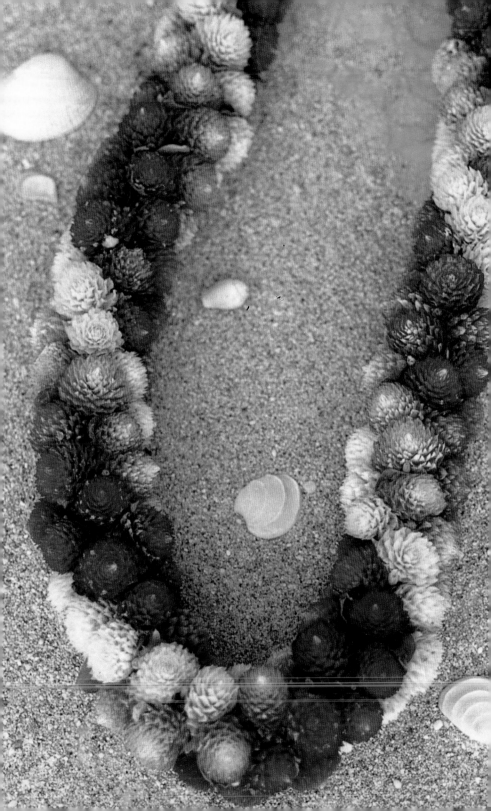

Lilia-O-Ka-Nile

Translation: Lily of the Nile • Common Name: Agapanthus, Blue Lily, African Lily, Lily of the Nile • Scientific Name: *Agapanthus praecox 'orientalis'* (lover flower, very early) Syn. *Agapanthus africanus* or *Agapanthus umbellatus* • Family Name: Lily (Liliaceae)

Description: A plant with grass-like leaves, blue or white blossoms, with 6 oblong petals, funnel-shaped, 1″ to 2″ long; borne on a large stalk of about 20-50 blossoms; no fragrance.

Characteristics: Rare blue color. One to four days lei life.

Climate/Location: Tropical climate; backyard cultivation; direct sunlight.

Season/Harvest Period: April through September. Pick blossoms in the early morning or evening when it is cool.

Quantity: About 75 blossoms for a 40″ single lei, *kui pololei,* straight pattern.

Storage: Sprinkle lightly. Place in plastic bag or container. Refrigerate.

Loke

Translation: Rose • Common Name: Rose, Damask Rose, or JB. • Scientific Name: *Rosa* spp. (rose) • Family Name: Rose (Rosaceae)

Description: A bush bearing 1″ long rose buds; light fragrance when in bloom.

Characteristics: The leaves may carry microscopic insect pests. The Federal Department of Agriculture prohibits this flower, with its leaves, to be taken to the Mainland. One to three days lei life.

Climate/Location: Tropical; warm climate; backyard cultivation; direct sunlight.

Season/Harvest Period: Year-round, peaking in summer. Pick blossoms early in the morning when in the tight bud stage.

Quantity: About 40 blossoms for a 40″ single lei, *kui pololei,* straight pattern.

Storage: Keep lei in a damp paper towel. Place in plastic bag or container. Refrigerate.

Loke Lau

Translation: Leaf Rose • Common Name: Green Rose • Scientific Name: *Rosa chinensis var. viridiflora* (rose, Chinese, with green flowers) • Family Name: Rose (Rosaceae)

Description: A shrub with green blossoms with narrow green leaves for petals, 1/2″ to 1″ in diameter; light spicy fragrance. The flower blossoms light green and darkens as it matures.

Characteristics: This flower may carry microscopic insect pests. The Federal Department of Agriculture prohibits any part of this plant to be taken to the Mainland. One to three days lei life.

Climate/Location: Warm climate; backyard cultivation; direct sunlight.

Season/Harvest Period: Year-round, less December through February. Pick in full-bloom.

Quantity: About 60 blossoms for a 40″ single lei, *kui pololei,* straight pattern.

Storage: Sprinkle lightly. Keep airtight. Place in plastic bag or container. Refrigerate.

Maile

Translation: Alyxia oliviformis • Common Name: Maile • Scientific Name: *Alyxia oliviformis* (chain, resembling the olive) • Family Name: Periwinkle or Plumeria (Apocynaceae)

Description: A vine with oval, pointed 1″ to 3″ long shiny leaves growing in pairs; bark and leaves have a vanilla-like fragrance.

Characteristics: A very popular open-ended horseshoe fashion lei; associated with Laka, Goddess of the Hula. One to four days lei life.

Climate/Location: Cool climate; found in native forests, commonly on the islands of Kaua'i and Hawai'i; indirect sunlight.

Season/Harvest Period: Year-round. Pick when cool.

Quantity: At one's discretion; averaging 15 vines.

Storage: Sprinkle lightly. Wrap in newspaper. Refrigerate.

Male

Translation: Marriage or Wedding • Common Name: Stephanotis • Scientific Name: *Marsdenia floribunda* Syn. *Stephanotis floribunda* (was flower, free-flowering) • Family Name: Milkweed or Crown Flower (Asclepiadaceae)

Description: A vine with fragrant, tubular, wax-white flowers; 1″ to 2″ long; 5 petals.

Characteristics: In old Hawai'i, the lei was sometimes worn by brides, thus the name "Male," meaning marriage. Today, it is a favorite in wedding bouquets. One to three days lei life.

Climate/Location: Warm climate; backyard cultivationon on fences; low elevation; direct sunlight.

Season/Harvest Period: March through November. Pick blossoms in the early morning or evening when cool.

Quantity: About 255 blossoms for a full, single lei, *kui pololei,* straight pattern.

Storage: Sprinkle lightly. Place in plastic bag or container. Refrigerate.

Melia

Translation: Plumeria • Common Name: Plumeria, Frangipani, or Graveyard Plumeria • Scientific Name: *Plumeria* spp. (named for Charles Plumier) • Family Name: Periwinkle (Apocynaceae)

Description: A tree with white and yellow blossoms about 2″ in diameter; five petals; fragrant.

Characteristics: Hybrid flowers found in a wide range of colors. One day lei life. The milky sap is poisonous if eaten.

Climate/Location: Warm climate; backyard cultivation; low elevation; direct sunlight.

Season/Harvest Period: Dormant during the winter, peaking in March through October.

Quantity: About 50 blossoms for a 40″ single lei, *kui pololei,* straight pattern.

Storage: Sprinkle lightly. Wrap in a damp paper or cloth towel. Place in the sink or bowl. Keep cool. Do not refrigerate.

Mokihana

Translation: Pelea anisata • Common Name: Mokihana • Scientific Name: *Pelea anisata* (named in honor of Pele, Goddess of the Volcano, like anise scented) • Family Name: Rue or Orange (Rutaceae)

Description: A tree with anise-scented, 1/2″ cube-shaped, leathery fruit. The fruit opens into two parts, hold 2 shiny black seeds in each section. Fruit color changes from green to brown.

Characteristics: The Mokihana lei represents the island of Kaua'i. Direct contact with bare, moist skin may cause a burn or irritation. The lei often serves as a sachet. The Federal Department of Agriculture prohibits the transportation of this fruit to the Mainland. Up to 20 days lei life if refrigerated.

Climate/Location: Warm climate; found only in the wild in tropical rainforests on the islands of Kaua'i and Hawai'i; direct sunlight.

Season/Harvest Period: May through September. Pick anytime. Fruit should be strung within a few hours of picking to prevent hardening.

Quantity: About 100 fruits for a 40″ single lei, *kui pololei,* straight pattern.

Storage: Wrap in damp newspaper. Place in plastic bag or container. Refrigerate.

Photo by David S. Boynton

Nani O 'Ōla'a

Translation: Beauty of 'Ōla'a (a city near Hilo, Hawaii) • Common Name: 'Ōla'a Beauty or Torenia • Scientific Name: *Torenia asiatica* (pretty annual named for Reverend Olof Toren, Asian) • Family Name: Snapdragon (Scrophulariaceae)

Description: A shrub with 1″ long dark violet, tubular blossoms with a yellow dotted corolla; no fragrance.

Characteristics: Fragile blossom. One day lei life.

Climate/Location: Warm climate. Grows wild in fields and along roadsides in 'Ōla'a, near Hilo, Hawai'i. Starter plants may be found in local garden shops for backyard cultivation; direct sunlight.

Season/Harvest Period: Year-round; abundant spring through summer. Water plants before picking blossoms; pick the blossoms early in the morning. Soak in water for a few minutes for firmness. Drain, then string.

Quantity: About 650 blossoms for a 40″ double lei, *kui poepoe,* circular pattern.

Storage: Keep dry and airtight. Wrap in dry tissue paper. Place in plastic bag or container. Refrigerate.

Nuku-ʻiʻiwi or Kaʻiʻiwi

Translation: Beak of the ʻIʻiwi Bird • Common Name: Jade • Scientific Name: *Strongylodon macrobotrys* (round tooth, with large grape-like clusters) • Family Name: Bean (Fabaceae)

Description: A vine with blue-green, 3-1/2″ long, unusual horny, pointed blossoms; no fragrance.

Characteristics: Prized for their bluish-green color, very rare in flowers. The seed attached to the base of the blossom may carry microscopic pests. The Federal Department of Agriculture prohibits transporting this flower to the Mainland. One to three days lei life.

Climate/Location: Warm climate; backyard cultivation; filtered sunlight.

Season/Harvest Period: Blossoms February through November. Pick blossoms early in the morning just after they open.

Quantity: About 95 blossoms for a 40″ flat lei, *kui lau,* back-and-forth pattern.

Storage: Sprinkle lightly. Fold or roll. Place in plastic bag or container. Refrigerate.

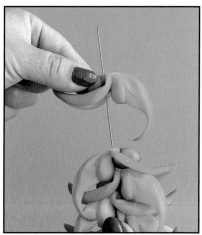

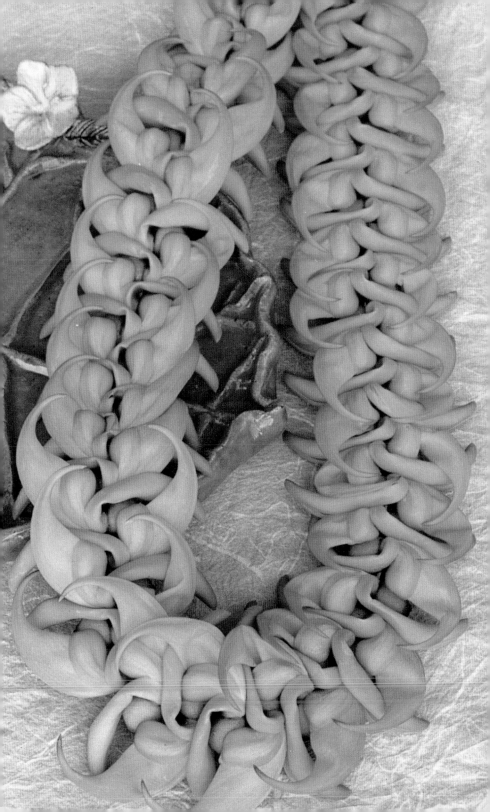

'Ohai Ali'i

Translation: Chief's Poinciana • Common Name: Dwarf Poinciana or Pride of Barbados • Scientific Name: *Caesalpinia pulcherrima* (ornamental trees and shrubs, named in honor of Andrea Cesalpini, pretty) • Family Name: Bean (Fabaceae)

Description: A shrub with red, pink, or yellow feather-like, wispy stamen blossoms, about 2″ in length; no fragrance.

Characteristics: The seed at the base of the blossom may carry microscopic insect pests. The Federal Department of Agriculture prohibits transporting this flower to the Mainland. One to three days lei life.

Climate/Location: Tropical, warm climate; backyard cultivation; direct sunlight.

Season/Harvest Period: Year-round, peaking from April through November. Pick blossoms fully opened, in the early morning when cool.

Quantity: About 360 blossoms for a 40″ double lei, *kui poepoe,* circular pattern.

Storage: Sprinkle lightly. Place in plastic bag or container. Refrigerate.

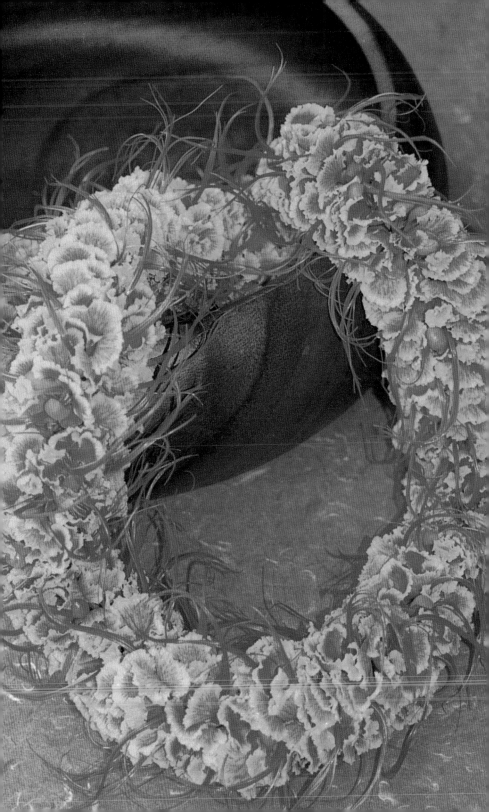

'Okika (Dendrobium) - Lavender

Translation: Orchid (Dendrobium) • Common Name: Lavender Dendrobium • Scientific Name: *Dendrobium* spp. (a tree, life) • Family Name: Orchid (Orchidaceae)

Description: A stalk-like plant with 2″ diameter blossoms with a lip, sepals and petals; light fragrance.

Characteristics: Hardy, long-lasting blossom with a tropical allure; blossoms in white, lavender, purple, green, and brown; popular for shipping to the Mainland. One to four days lei life.

Climate/Location: Tropical, warm climate; backyard cultivation; indirect or direct sunlight.

Season/Harvest Period: Year-round, however, some varieties do not blossom in quantity during winter. Pick when cool and blossoms are fully opened.

Quantity: About 60 blossoms for a 40″ single lei, *kui pololei,* straight pattern.

Storage: Sprinkle lightly. Place in a plastic bag or container. Refrigerate. May be revived by soaking in cold water in the refrigerator for four hours; shake off excess water. Place in a plastic bag. Refrigerate.

'Okika (Dendrobium) - Thailand

Translation: Orchid (Dendrobium) • Common Name: Dendrobium, Soniya Red, Bom or Thailand Dendrobium • Scientific Name: *Dendrobium hybrids* (a tree, life) • Family Name: Orchid (Orchidaceae)

Description: A stalk-like plant with 2″ to 3″ diameter blossoms with a noticeable lip; sepals and petals; light fragrance.

Characteristics: Hardy, long-lasting blossom with a tropical allure; blossoms in lavenderish-purple; popular for shipping to the Mainland. One to four days lei life.

Climate/Location: Tropical, warm climate; backyard cultivation; indirect or direct sunlight.

Season/Harvest Period: Year-round. Pick when cool and blossoms are fully opened.

Quantity: About 50 blossoms for a 40″ single lei, *kui pololei,* straight pattern.

Storage: Sprinkle lightly. Place in a plastic bag or container. Refrigerate. May be revived by soaking in cold water in the refrigerator for four hours; shake off excess water. Place in a plastic bag. Refrigerate.

'Okika (Epidendrum) - Hōkūle'a

Translation: Orchid (Epidendrum) A Zenith star above Hawai'i • Common Name: Epidendrum, Epis, or Baby Orchid • Scientific Name: *Epidendrum 'Hokulea'* (upon a tree, epiphytic or tree-perching orchids) • Family Name: Orchid (Orchidaceae)

Description: A grass-like stemmed plant with numerous clustered, orange blossoms; no fragrance.

Characteristics: Epis come in a variety of colors; usually the reds and oranges are used for leis. One to three days lei life.

Climate/Location: Warm climate; backyard cultivation; direct or indirect sunlight.

Season/Harvest Period: Year-round, peaking in the spring through summer. Pick blossoms when they are fully opened. Pick when cool.

Quantity: About 350 blossoms for a 40″ double lei, *kui poepoe,* circular pattern.

Storage: Sprinkle lightly. Refrigerate.

'Okika Lepo (Ground)

Translation: Ground Orchid • Common Name: Ground Orchid, or Philipine Wind Orchid • Scientific Name: *Spathoglottis plicata* (a tongue like a spade, with pleated leaves) • Family Name: Orchid (Orchidaceae)

Description: A short plant, about 2′ tall, with wide, long, drooping leaves, having numerous clustered, purple blossoms with a touch of yellow deep in its throat. Mild fragrance.

Characteristics: Hardy, long-lasting blossom. One to four days lei life.

Climate/Location: Warm climate; found growing cultivated and in the wild in open grassy fields; direct sunlight.

Season/Harvest Period: Year-round; peaking in the spring through summer. Pick the blossoms in the early to mid-morning when cool.

Quantity: About 275 blossoms for a 40″ double lei, *kui pololei,* circular pattern.

Storage: Sprinkle lightly. Place in a plastic bag or container. Refrigerate.

'Okika (Vanda)

Translation: Orchid (Vanda) • Common Name: Vanda, Miss Joaquim, or Vanda Orchid • Scientific Name: *Vanda 'Miss Joaquim'* (Hindi name for one epiphytic orchid, named after Miss Joaquim) • Family Name: Orchid (Orchidaceae)

Description: An erect vine with purplish, 2-1/2″ diameter blossoms with a noticeable lobed lip, 3 rounded lavender petals, and 2 rounded white sepals; mild fragrance.

Characteristics: Strong and durable; popular for shipping to the Mainland. One to five days lei life.

Climate/Location: Warm to cool climate; backyard cultivation; direct sunlight.

Season/Harvest Period: Year-round, peaking in the summer. Pick blossoms in the evening or early morning when it is cool.

Quantity: About 50 blossoms for a 40″ single lei, *kui pololei,* straight pattern.

Storage: Sprinkle well. Wrap in damp newspaper or paper towel. Store in a paper box. Flowers may turn white if kept airtight. Refrigerate. May be revived by soaking in cold water in the refrigerator for four hours; shake off excess water. Place in a plastic bag. Refrigerate.

Pahūpahū

Translation: Firecracker • Common Name: Firecracker, Flame Vine, or Firecracker Vine • Scientific Name: *Manettia luteo-rubra 'Paraguariensis'* (ornamental twining plants named for *Saverio Manetti*-yellowish-red) • Family Name: Coffee (Rubiaceae)

Description: A vine with 1″ long bright red, slender, fuzzy blossoms; no fragrance.

Characteristics: Attractive, bright color. One to two days lei life.

Climate/Location: Tropical climate; backyard cultivation; direct sunlight.

Season/Harvest Period: Year-round. Pick blossoms early in the morning or evening when cool.

Quantity: About 450 blossoms for a 40″ double lei, *kui poepoe,* circular pattern.

Storage: Keep dry. Place in plastic bag or container. Refrigerate.

Pakalana

Translation: Paklan • Common Name: Chinese Violet • Scientific Name: *Telosma cordata* (far fragrance, heart-shaped) • Family Name: Milkweed or Crownflower (Asclepiadaceae)

Description: A vine with 1″ long, tubular, yellowish-green, five-part blossoms; strong fragrance.

Characteristics: Lei associated with "love." One to two days lei life.

Climate/Location: Tropical, warm climate; backyard cultivation; grown on a fence or trellis; direct sunlight.

Season/Harvest Period: Abundant May through October. Pick blossoms early in the morning when cool. Place in plastic container until enough blossoms have been collected. Refrigerate.

Quantity: About 135 blossoms for a 40″ single lei, *kui pololei,* straight pattern.

Storage: Sprinkle. Place in a damp paper towel. Store in a plastic bag or container. Refrigerate. May be revived by soaking in cold water in the refrigerator for four hours; shake off excess water. Place in a plastic bag. Refrigerate.

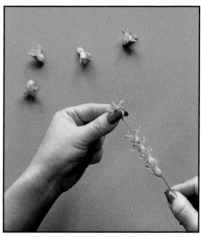

Pīkake

Translation: Peacock • Common Name: Arabian Jasmine or Sampaguita • Scientific Name: *Jasminum sambac* (Persian for yasmin, sweet scented shrub and climbers, Zambac Persian name for Jasmine) • Family Name: Olive (Oleaceae)

Description: A shrub with small, white, tubular, pearl-like, 3/4″ long buds. The fully opened flowers are about 1″ in diameter with 5 to 9 petals; intensely fragrant.

Characteristics: Popular wedding flower lei in Hawai'i. The buds start to blossom immediately when not refrigerated. One day lei life.

Climate/Location: Tropical, hot, dry climate; low elevation; back-yard cultivation; direct sunlight.

Season/Harvest Period: Year-round, less in December through February. Pick early in the morning as buds. Place in a sealed glass jar. Refrigerate until enough buds have been collected.

Quantity: About 100 blossoms for a 40″ single lei, *kui pololei,* straight pattern.

Storage: Keep dry. Coil lei in a flat, spiral pattern. Wrap in wax paper. Refrigerate.

Poni-Mō'ī

Translation: Coronation • Common Name: Carnation • Scientific Name: *Dianthus caryophyllus* (Zeus flower or flower of love, smell of walnut leaves) • Family Name: Pink (Caryophyllaceae)

Description: A plant with 3″ diameter blossoms consisting of 30 or more petals forming a round head; edges are toothed; cylindrical calyx is 5-toothed; mild fragrance.

Characteristics: There are large numbers of species and hybrids. A popular lei for graduation. One to three days lei life.

Climate/Location: Cool, upland climate; backyard cultivation; direct sunlight.

Season/Harvest Period: Year-round, less in December through February. Pick blossoms early in the morning when cool.

Quantity: About 70 blossoms for a full single lei, *kui pololei,* straight pattern.

Storage: Sprinkle well; gently shake off excess water. Wrap in a damp paper towel. Store in a plastic bag. Refrigerate. Shake off excess water before wearing.

Poni-Mō'ī (Iki)

Translation: Small Coronation • Common Name: Mini Carnation, Pixie Carnation • Scientific Name: *Dianthus caryophyllus* (Zeus flower or flower of love, smell of walnut leaves) • Family Name: Pink (Caryophyllaceae)

Description: A plant with 2″ diameter blossoms, have sprays of 5-6 flowers per stem, consisting of 30 or more petals forming a round head; edges are toothed; cylindrical calyx is 5-toothed; mild fragrance.

Characteristics: Hybrid flowers, found in a wide range of colors. They are single or double with feathery petals. A popular lei for visitors arriving and departing the Islands. One to three days lei life.

Climate/Location: Cool, upland climate; backyard cultivation; direct sunlight.

Season/Harvest Period: Year-round, less in December through February. Pick blossoms early in the morning when cool.

Quantity: About 40 blossoms for a single lei, *kui pololei,* straight pattern.

Storage: Store in a plastic bag or container. Refrigerate.

Pōpō Lehua

Translation: Ixora • Common Name: Ixora • Scientific Name: *Ixora casei* (from the Portuguese Israra - refering to the god Siva, named after a person "Casei") • Family Name: Coffee (Rubiaceae)

Description: A shrub grown ornamentally for its large round clusters of red flowers. Flowers are about 1″ in diameter with a long, narrow corona. No fragrance.

Characteristics: There are other species of Ixora, but Ixora casei is best for lei-making. One to four days lei life.

Climate/Location: Warm climate; backyard cultivation; direct sunlight.

Season/Harvest Period: Year-round. Pick blossoms when they are fully opened, in the morning when cool.

Quantity: About 240 blossoms for a 40″ single lei, *kui pololei*, straight pattern.

Storage: Keep dry. Place in a plastic bag or container. Refrigerate.

Waina Kai

Translation: Sea Grape • Common Name: Sea Grape • Scientific Name: *Coccoloba uvifera* (seaside grape, bearing grape) • Family Name: Buckwheat (Polygonaceae)

Description: A tree bearing light green, edible, pear-shaped fruit hanging in clusters resembling grape clusters. No fragrance.

Characteristics: This fruit may carry microscopic insect pests. The Federal Department of Agriculture prohibits transporting this fruit lei to the Mainland. Up to seven days lei life.

Climate/Locaation: Warm climate; low elevation; near sandy shores; direct sunlight.

Season/Harvest Period: Abundant from April through November. Harvest anytime.

Quantity: About 80 fruits for a 40″ single lei, *kui pololei,* straight pattern.

Storage: Keep dry. Place in plastic bag or container. Refrigerate.

LEI RESTRICTIONS

The Federal Department of Agriculture will not allow leis from the following flowers, foliage and fruits to enter the U.S. Mainland:

- Hala – Screw Pine
  Pandanus techorius

- Hinahina 'Umi 'Umi O Dole –
  Spanish Moss
  Tillandsia usneoides

- Kākia – Cassia or Candle Bush
  Senna alata

- Kauhi – True Maunaloa
  Canavalia cathartica

- Kauna'oa – Dodder
  Cuscuta sandwichiana

- Kiele – Gardenia
  Gardenia augusta

- Kiele (Peke) – Dwarf Gardenia
  Gardenia augusta 'radicans'

- Kīkānia – Solanum
  Solanum capsicoides

- Loke – Rose with Leaves

  Rosa damascena

- Loke Lau – Green Rose
  Rosa chinensis var. viridiflora

- Maile (if insect pest are visible)
  Alyxia oliviformis

- Mokihana
  Pelea anisata

- Nuku'i'iwi – Jade
  Strongylodon macrobotrys

- 'Ohai Ali'i – Dwarf Poinciana
  Caesalpina pulcherrima

- Waina Kai – Sea Grape
  Coccoloba uvifera

- All "Pea subfamily"
  (any part of the plant)

- All berries and fruits

For more information, call the United States
Department of Agriculture, (808) 861-8490
(listing is subject to change).

BIBLIOGRAPHY

Bird, Arden J., and Josephine Puninani Kanekoa Bird. *Hawaiian Flower Lei Making*. Honolulu: University of Hawaii Press, 1987.

Clay, Horace F., and Hubbard, James C. *The Hawaiian Graden Tropical Shrubs*. Honolulu; University of Hawaii Press, 1977.

Clay, Horace F., and Hubbard, James C. *The Hawaiian Garden Torpical Exotics*. Honolulu: University of Hawaii Press, 1977.

Coombes, Allen J. *Dictionary of Plant Names*. Portland, Oregon: Timber Press, 1985.

Hargreaves, Dorothy. *Tropical Blossoms of the Pacific*. Honolulu: Hargreaves Co., 1970.

Kuck, Lorraine E. *Hawaiian Flowers and Flowering Trees*. Ruthland, Vermont: E. Tuttle Company, Inc., 1958.

Kuck, Lorraine E. *The Story of the Lei*. Honolulu: Tongg Publishing Co., 1983.

McDonald, Marie A. *Ka Lei: The Leis of Hawaii*. Honolulu: Press Pacifica, 1989.

Moir, May A. *The Garden Watcher, Revised Edition*. Honolulu: University of Hawaii Press, Bishop Museum Press, 1989.

Neal, Bill. *Gardener's Latin*. Chapel Hill, North Carolina: Algonquin Books of Chapel Hill; a division of Workman Publishing Company Inc., 1992.

Neal, Marie C. *In Gardens of Hawaii*. Honolulu: Bishop Museum Press, 1965.

Pukui, Mary Kawena, and Elbert, Samuel H. *Hawaiian Dictionary, Revised and Enlarged Edition*. Honolulu: University of Hawaii Press, 1986.

Smith, A.W. *A Gardener's Dictionary of Plant Names*. New York: St. Martin's Press, 1972.

Wagner, Warren L., Herbst, Derral R., and Sohmer, S.H. *Manual of the Flowering Plants of Hawaii, Volume 1*. Honolulu: University of Hawaii Press, Bishop Museum Press, 1990.

Wagner, Warren L., Herbst, Derral R., and Sohmer, S.H. *Manual of the Flowering Plants of Hawaii, Volume 2*. Honolulu: University of Hawaii Press, Bishop Museum Press, 1990.